Timeless Knits for Kids
(Size 4-14)

Chris de Longpré

Timeless Knits Publications, Kentwood, Michigan, U.S.A.

Photography: Chris de Longpré
Book design and production: Janel Laidman

Timeless Knits Publications, a division of
Knitting At KNoon Designs, LLC
P.O. Box 8453
Kentwood, MI 49518

e-mail: Chris@TimelessKnitsPublications.com
website: TimelessKnitsPublications.com

Printed in North America by Friesens, Manitoba, Canada

For

Alux, Jaremay, Elyzabeth, and Caleb

Twenty-something years ago you
Tenderly gazed
Into her tiny face
And your heart swelled.
So much love! You never imagined you could feel this way.
Until,

Several years later you
Tenderly gazed
Into another tiny face
And your heart continued to swell.
You never imagined you
Could feel this way
Again.

Day by day,
Year by year
You watched them grow.
In the blink of an eye
They were no longer tiny,
No longer needful.

Soon, you will rush to the hospital
And gaze into your daughter's face,
And your heart will swell to new proportions.
Then you'll tenderly gaze
Into a new tiny face,
And your heart will ache with the swell.
So much love
Again!

Day by day,
Year by year
You will watch them grow,
The mother and the child.
You, the lucky grandmother, get to experience
Love squared.

—Chris de Longpré, 2002

Contents

Introduction

For longer than I can remember I have been making things. My grandmother used to tell a story about the time I visited with my grandparents for a week while my first younger sister was being born. Every day after lunch my grandmother would sit down to sew for a while before she had to get busy with dinner preparation. As the story goes, whenever she got out her sewing, I asked for "terial." We both grew quite frustrated because she could not figure out what I wanted. Some time during the visit she must have talked to my parents by phone, because she figured out that what I wanted was material. I wanted to make things, too. My mother kept me busy with scraps of material while she was sewing and I wanted to do the same at my grandmother's house.

One of the reasons that knitting for children is so satisfying is that kids are always making things. They use whatever materials are at hand to make forts, mud pies, treasure maps, pictures of all sorts, and various constructed pieces that are sometimes hard to identify. Along with making things, they like to give them to those they love. When you take the time to knit for kids, they notice.

My four grandchildren, who also model the sweaters in the photos, inspired the designs in this book. I knit every stitch of every sweater they are wearing in the photos. The patterns have also been test knit and other samples have been made, but I wanted the children to have the sweaters to keep as soon as I finished each photo session, and I wanted them to know that I knit their sweaters with love. I also did all the photography for this book, making this project a highly personal journey. For me, it's only 75% about knitting. It's at least 25% photo album, and it's 100% from my heart.

The designs are timeless; they could have been worn by me, my brother, and my sisters half a century ago; they could have been worn by my daughters a generation ago; my grandchildren are wearing them today; and I trust that these patterns will still be useful 20 and 50 years from now. I've used basic techniques and presented each sweater in a wide range of sizes to fit children from the end of toddlerhood through late childhood. Included are pullovers, vests, and cardigans to suit the tastes of both girls and boys. There are both top-down and bottom-up architectures, with modified T, raglan, saddle shoulder, and set-in sleeves; all with minimized sewing. These basics will prove to be useful in any child's wardrobe, and, because they are timeless, they can be handed down from child to child for many years.

When you make the sweaters in this book for the children in your lives, you'll be giving them the greatest gift possible – you'll be wrapping them in love.

Chris de Longpré
October 2009

Summer Camp 2008

Secrets for Successful Fit

These might not be secrets, exactly, but if the chapter title inspired you to read it, that was the point. I've seen my share of misshapen, ill-fitting knitted sweaters. I've also been asked questions about row gauge and how to modify a pattern to fit. The material that follows seems quite basic, but I am always delightfully surprised by the lights that go on when I present this material to a knitting group.

Gauge

No discussion of fit and knitting can possibly proceed without discussion of the dreaded "g" word – gauge. Before your eyes glaze over and you flip to a new page, please be assured that you cannot possibly hope to knit garments that fit until you *really* understand the role that gauge plays.

I've many times heard a knitter say, "I always get gauge." It's a wonderful statement if it means that the knitter never proceeds to cast on a project without first working as many gauge swatches as necessary to match the gauge the designer achieved when writing the pattern. I suspect, however, that many knitters just pick up the needle size indicated in the pattern, cast on, and merrily knit away, *hoping* that their gauge will be *close*. There are many reasons why this approach is a gamble that will most often result in an ill-fitting garment. Let's talk about some of those reasons.

Why does gauge matter?

Consider this example: You are going to knit a sweater for your grandson. The pattern gauge calls for 20 sts and 24 rows over 4" in stockinet stitch. Dividing each dimension by 4, you see that that is 5 sts and 6 rows per inch. You knit a swatch and your first measurement indicates that you have 5¼ sts per inch. Maybe if you just stretch it a bit it seems like 5 sts per inch. So you decide that's good enough. You cast on 130 sts for a sweater that should have a circumference of 26";

13" when measured flat. After knitting the first seven or eight inches, you decide to measure and you discover that your sweater is only about 12¼" when measured flat, or 24½" in circumference. That not-insignificant ¼ st at gauge swatching time can grow into quite a significant sizing problem.

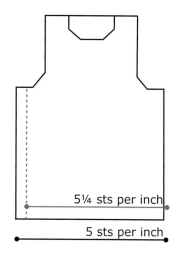

The oops factor: ¼ st per inch off gauge

As you forged ahead, you also neglected to check your row gauge. Now it is time to knit the sleeves. Had you checked the swatch for row gauge, you would have seen that you were knitting at 5½ rows per inch instead of 6 rows per inch. The instructions for shaping along the length of the sleeve call for an increase on each side every 6th row 5 times and then every 4th row 13 times more. Gracious, if your row gauge is off you may not even know how to arrive at sleeves that are the correct length.

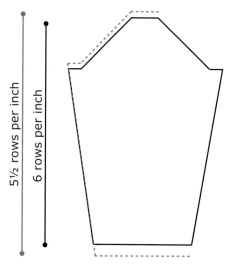

The oops factor: ½ row per inch off gauge

Camp Jacket, p.26

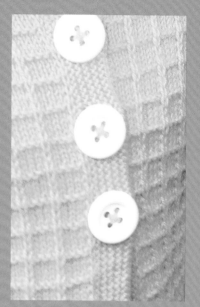

Tic-Tac-Toe, p.34

Willow, p.42

Beachcomber, p.50

Old Sport, p.58

Vested, p.66

Cotton Candy, p.74

Head of the Class, p.82

Rib Tickler, p.90

Skip, p.96

Turtle, p.104

Xander, p.112

Camp Jacket

Near the end of every summer my husband and I, together with our daughters, grandchildren, and various friends and dogs, gather at a cottage in northern Michigan for what we call Summer Camp. It's a week filled with swimming, row boating, kayaking, kite flying, dune climbing, blueberry picking, campfires, and whatever else we find to enjoy before we run out of time. Many traditions have emerged from this family week, and one of them is the camp jacket. Its oversized fit, modified drop shoulders, and soft hand make it as easy and comfortable to wear as a hooded sweatshirt.

Measurements

Size	4	6	8	10	12	14
Child's Chest	23″	25″	27″	28″	30″	32″
Finished Sweater:						
Chest	30″	32″	34″	35″	37″	39″
Cross Back (shoulder to shoulder)	12½″	13½″	15″	15″	15″	16½″
Center Back Neck to Cuff	20¼″	21½″	23″	25″	26½″	27¾″

Materials

Yarn

885 (1020, 1175, 1275, 1450, 1635) yards worsted weight. Model is shown in Tatamy Tweed Worsted, by Kraemer Yarns, 5 (6, 7, 7, 8, 9) balls, Pumpkin Tweed.

Needles

24″ circular needle, US size 7 (4.5 mm), or size needed to obtain gauge; 24″ circular needle and 2 double-point needles one size smaller for placket and hood trim, and for I-cord ties.

Other

Stitch markers, stitch holders, tapestry needle

Gauge

20 sts and 24 rows = 4″ in stockinet stitch

Notes

1) Please read the Notes, Techniques, and Abbreviations section, p. 120, before you begin.

2) Sweater body is worked in the round from hem to placket opening, and then worked back and forth as one piece to the underarms. The back and fronts are worked separately above the underarms. Sleeves are worked flat from stitches picked up at armhole edges, then seamed and joined to body at underarms. The hood is worked up from stitches picked up along the neck edge. Hood and placket trim are knitted on last. I-cord ties are made separately and sewn on.

Pattern stitches

Edging, worked in the round (for jacket body)

Round 1 (RS)   knit
Round 2   knit
Round 3 (ridge) purl
Round 4   knit
Round 5   knit
Round 6   knit
Round 7 (ridge) purl
Work rounds 1–7; rep rounds 4-7, three times more.

Edging, worked flat (for sleeves)

Row 1 (WS) purl
Row 2 knit
Row 3 (ridge) knit
Row 4 knit
Row 5 purl
Row 6 knit
Row 7 (ridge) knit

Work rows 1-7; rep rows 4-7, three times more. Knit one row. Purl one row. BO loosely in knit.

Instructions

Cast on at hem: With larger needle, CO 150 (160, 170, 176, 186, 196) sts. Join in a round, PM, and work edging. Continue in stockinet stitch until jacket measures 11½" (12¼", 13", 14½", 15½", 17") from cast-on round.

Divide for placket: On the next round, knit 36 (38, 41, 42, 45, 47) sts. BO 3 (4, 3, 4, 3, 4) sts at center front. Knit to end (at center front). Turn. Work flat in stockinet stitch until jacket measures 13" (14", 15", 16", 17", 18") from cast-on round, ending ready to work a RS row.

Divide back and fronts: Knit 30 (32, 35, 36, 36, 38); BO 12 (12, 12, 12, 18, 18); k 62 (67, 72, 75, 74, 79); BO 12 (12, 12, 12, 18, 18); k to end. There will be 63 (68, 73, 76, 75, 80) sts for the back and 30 (32, 35, 36, 36, 38) sts for each front section.

Left front: Work even until left front measures 3½" (3¾", 4", 4½", 5", 6") above underarm bind-off row, ending ready to work a WS row. Front placket opening will measure 5" (5½", 6", 6", 6½", 7"). BO 5 (6, 6, 6, 6, 7) sts, purl to end. Decrease 1 st at neck edge every RS row 7 (6, 7, 7, 7, 7) times, as follows: k to last 3 sts, k2tog, k1. Work even on 18 (20, 22, 23, 23, 24) sts, as necessary, until arm-hole measures 6" (6 ½", 7", 7½", 8", 9") above underarm bind-off row. Place 18 (20, 22, 23, 23, 24) sts on a stitch holder for left front shoulder.

Right front: Beginning at center front, work even until right front measures 3½" (3¾", 4", 4½", 5", 6") above underarm bind-off row, ending ready to work a RS row. Front placket opening will measure 5" (5½", 6", 6", 6½", 7"). BO 5 (6, 6, 6, 6, 7) sts, knit to end. Decrease 1 st at neck edge every RS row 7 (6, 7, 7, 7, 7) times, as follows: k1, ssk, k to end. Work

even on 18 (20, 22, 23, 23, 24) sts, as necessary, until armhole measures 6" (6½", 7", 7½", 8", 9") above underarm bind-off row. Place 18 (20, 22, 23, 23, 24) sts on a stitch holder for right front shoulder.

Back: Beginning with a RS row, work even until armhole measures 6" (6½", 7", 7½", 8", 9") above underarm bind-off row, ending ready to work a RS row. Knit across 18 (20, 22, 23, 23, 24) sts, and place them on a stitch holder for right shoulder. BO center 27 (28, 29, 30, 29, 32) sts. Knit to end, placing 18 (20, 22, 23, 23, 24) sts on a stitch holder for left shoulder.

Join shoulders with the three-needle bind-off technique. Weave in ends. Block jacket body.

Sleeves: With RS facing, using larger needle, leaving underarm bound-off sts free, pick up and knit 60 (65, 70, 75, 80, 90) sts along the long armhole edge. Continue in stockinet stitch, decreasing 1 st each side, every 6th row 9 (7, 3, 7, 10, 5) times, and then every 4th row 1 (5, 12,

9, 7, 15) times as follows: k2, ssk, k to last 4 sts, k2tog, k2. Work even in stockinet stitch on 40 (41, 40, 43, 46, 50) sts until sleeve, when measured at center, is 10½"(11¼", 12", 14", 15½", 16"). Work edging at cuff. Repeat for second sleeve.

Block armhole seams and sleeves, if desired.

Sew one-half of the bound-off underarm sts to the top front edge of one sleeve. Sew the other half of the bound-off underarm sts to the top back edge of the sleeve. Sew long under-sleeve seam. Repeat for second sleeve.

Hood: With RS facing, using larger needle, pick up and knit 70 (74, 80, 82, 82, 86) sts. Work a WS increase row as follows: p10 (12, 14, 14, 14, 16), pfb in the next 5 sts, p40 (40, 42, 44, 44, 44), pfb in the next 5 sts, p to end. Work even in stockinet stitch on 80 (84, 90, 92, 92, 96) sts, until hood measures 10½" (11", 11", 12", 12", 13"), ending ready to work a WS row. Purl 40 (42, 45, 46, 46, 48), to center back of hood. Fold hood with RS together and join the center top with the three-needle bind-off technique.

Block hood, if desired.

Trim: With smaller needle, from the RS, beginning at the bottom of the placket, pick up and knit sts along the right front placket edge, around the face edge of the hood, and along the left front placket edge. (Pick up and knit sts at a ratio of 5 sts for every 6 rows, decreasing the ratio to 3 sts for every 6 rows for 2" to 3" either side of the center top hood seam.) Work trim back and forth in garter stitch for 7 rows. BO loosely in knit.

Sew the bottom of the left front trim edge to the bottom of the placket opening. Sew the bottom of the right front placket trim behind the left front trim to the seam at the bottom of the placket.

Ties: With 2 double-pointed needles, work 2, 8" lengths of 3-st I-cord. Attach ties where the trim meets the front edges, 2" to 3" below the neckline/hood seam.

Finishing: Weave in ends.

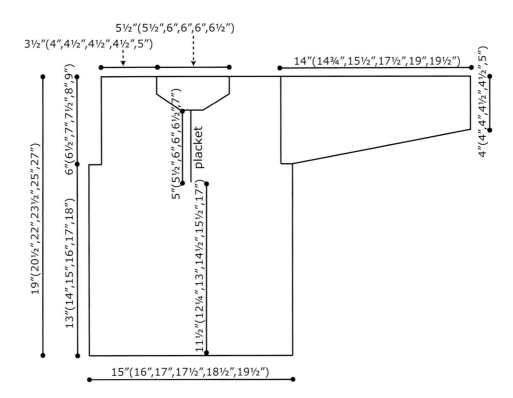

5½"(5½",6",6",6",6½")

3½"(4",4½",4½",4½",5")

14"(14¾",15½",17½",19",19½")

4"(4",4",4½",4½",5")

6"(6½",7",7½",8",9")

5"(5½",6",6½",7")

placket

19"(20½",22",23½",25",27")

13"(14",15",16",17",18")

11½"(12¼",13",14½",15½",17")

15"(16",17",17½",18½",19½")

Tic-Tac-Toe

Not your traditional schoolgirl cardigan, for a not-your-traditional girl. A fun, checked pattern pairs with ribbing and oversized buttons, shown here in a bright, sunny color. Modified drop shoulders and a loose fit allow this sweater to serve double-duty as a great jacket for early fall and late spring.

Measurements

Size	4	6	8	10	12	14
Child's Chest	23″	25″	27″	28″	30″	32″
Finished Sweater:						
Chest	27″	28½″	31½″	32″	34″	36″
Cross Back (shoulder to shoulder)	11½″	12½″	13½″	13½″	14″	14½″
Center Back Neck to Cuff	20″	21¼″	22″	24″	26″	26¾″

Materials

Yarn

650 (750, 875, 1000, 1175, 1325) yards worsted weight. Model is shown in Encore Worsted, by Plymouth Yarn, 4 (4, 5, 5, 6, 7) balls, color number 1382.

Needles

24″ circular needle, US size 8 (5.0 mm), or size needed to obtain gauge; and 16″ or 24″ circular needle one size smaller for trim

Other

Stitch markers, stitch holders, tapestry needle, and 3, 1½″ buttons

Gauge

22 sts and 28 rows = 4″ in overall pattern stitch (for body)

22 sts and 26 rows = 4″ in ribbing pattern (for sleeves)

Notes

1) Please read the Notes, Techniques, and Abbreviations section, p. 120, before you begin.

2) Sweater body is worked flat, as one piece, from hem to underarms, then divided to work back and fronts separately. Sleeves are worked flat from stitches picked up at armhole edges, then seamed and joined to body at underarms. Collar, hem, and button bands are knitted on last.

Pattern Stitches

Overall pattern stitch (body)

Row 1 (RS) k1, *sl1, k4, rep from *, across, ending sl1, k1
Row 2 purl
Row 3 rep row 1
Row 4 purl
Row 5 rep row 1
Row 6 (WS) p2, *k4, p1, rep from *, across, ending k4, p2

Ribbing stitch (sleeves)

Row 1 (WS) p4, *k1, p4, rep from * across
Row 2 k4, *p1, k4, rep from * across

Instructions

Cast on at hem: With larger needle, CO 148 (158, 173, 178, 188, 198) sts.

Body: Begin with row 6 of overall pattern stitch (WS). Then repeat rows 1-6 until sweater measures 10" (10½", 12". 13½", 15", 15") from cast-on edge, ending ready to work row 1 or row 3.

Divide for back and fronts: Work across the first 31 (33, 36, 36, 38, 40) sts in established pattern. Keeping those sts on the right-hand needle for right front, BO 11 (12, 13, 16, 17, 18). Work to end in established pattern. Turn. Purl across the first 31 (33, 36, 36, 38, 40) sts. Keeping those sts on the right-hand needle for left front, BO 11 (12, 13, 16, 17, 18). Purl across remaining sts for back. There will be 64 (68, 75, 74, 78, 82) sts for the back and 31 (33, 36, 36, 38, 40) sts for each front section.

Back: Work in established pattern until back measures 6" (6½", 7", 7½", 8", 9") above underarm bind-off row, ending ready to work row 3 or 5. On the next

row knit 18 (19, 22, 22, 22, 23) sts and place them on a stitch holder for right shoulder. BO 28 (30, 31, 30, 34, 36) sts for center back neck. Knit to end, placing remaining 18 (19, 22, 22, 22, 23) sts on a stitch holder for left shoulder.

Right front: Beginning with a WS row, purl across sts for right front. Continue working in established pattern until right front measures 4" (4", 4½", 5", 5½", 6") above underarm bind-off row, ending ready to work row 1 or 3. BO 9 (10, 10, 10, 12, 13) sts at center front and work to the end of the row in established pattern. Continue in established pattern, decreasing 1 st at neck edge every RS row 4 times, as follows: ssk, work in established pattern to end.

Right shoulder: Continue working in established pattern on 18 (19, 22, 22, 22, 23) sts until right front armhole measures 6" (6½", 7", 7½", 8", 9") above underarm bind-off row, ending ready to work row 3 or 5, to match back. Knit across stitches for right shoulder and place them on a stitch holder.

Left front: Beginning with a RS row, work across sts for left front. Continue working in established pattern until left front measures 4" (4", 4½", 5", 5½", 6") above underarm bind-off row, ending ready to work row 2 or 4. BO 9 (10, 10, 10, 12, 13) sts at center front and purl to the end of the row. Continue in established pattern, decreasing 1 st at neck edge every RS row 4 times, as follows: work in established pattern to last 2 sts, k2tog.

Left shoulder: Continue working in established pattern on 18 (19, 22, 22, 22, 23) sts until left front armhole measures 6" (6½", 7", 7½", 8", 9") above underarm bind-off row, ending ready to work row 3 or 5, to match back and right front. Knit across stitches for left shoulder and place them on a stitch holder.

Join shoulders with the three-needle bind-off technique.

Sleeves: With RS facing, and larger needle, leaving underarm bound-off stitches free, pick up and knit 64 (74, 79, 84, 89, 99) sts along the long armhole edge.

Beginning with a WS row, work in ribbing pattern for sleeves, decreasing 1 st each side every 6th row 7 (3, 4, 6, 6, 8) times, then every 4th row 8 (15, 14, 14, 17, 15) times, maintaining established pattern, as follows: ssk, work to last 2 sts, k2tog. Work even in established pattern on 34 (38, 43, 44, 43, 53) sts until sleeve, when measured at center, is 12¼" (13", 13¼", 15¼", 17", 17½"). Switch to smaller needle and continue in established pattern for 1¾" more, ending ready to work a WS row. Work one row in reverse of established pattern (knit instead of purl, purl instead of knit). BO loosely in knit.

Sew one-half of the bound-off underarm sts to the top front edge of one sleeve. Sew the other half of the bound-off underarm sts to the top back edge of the sleeve. Sew long under-sleeve seam. Repeat for second sleeve.

Add collar: From the WS (with wrong side of sweater facing), beginning at upper left neck edge, with larger needle, pick up and knit sts along the neck edge (see Techniques section, p. 121), adjusting to a multiple of 5 sts plus 1. Work collar, as follows, for 3″ (3″, 3″, 3½″, 3½″, 4″):

Row 1 (RS) k1, *p4, k1, rep from * across
Row 2 p1, *k4, p1, rep from * across

Repeat these 2 rows for collar, ending ready to work a WS row. Work row 1 of pattern from the WS. BO loosely in knit.

Add hem: From the RS, with smaller needle, pick up and knit 148 (158, 173, 178, 188, 198) sts along the cast-on edge. Work the following pattern, alternating rows, for 5 rows:

Row 1 (WS) k2, p4, *k1, p4, rep from * across, ending k2
Row 2 p2, k4, *p1, k4, rep from * across, ending p2

BO. Turn hem to inside and sew in place with a gentle tension, leaving ends along center fronts open.

Add button bands

Right front band (buttonholes): From the RS, with smaller needle, pick up and knit stitches along the center front at a ratio of 3 sts for every 4 rows. Work as follows:

Row 1 (WS) k12, PM, k15, PM, k15, PM, knit to the end of the row
Row 2 *k to marker, remove marker, BO 5, rep from *, ending by knitting to the end of the row
Row 3 *k to BO, turn, use the cable cast-on to cast on 5 sts, turn, rep from *, ending by knitting to the end of the row
Rows 4-9 knit

BO loosely.

Left front band: Pick up and knit sts along the center front, as for right front band. Work in garter stitch for 9 rows. BO loosely.

Finishing: Sew buttons to left front band opposite buttonholes in right front band. Weave in ends and block.

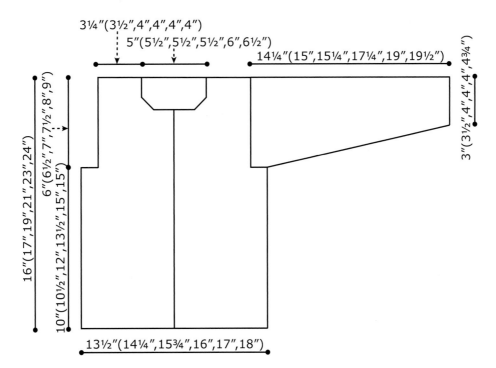

3¼"(3½",4",4",4",4")

5"(5½",5½",5½",6",6½")

14¼"(15",15¼",17¼",19",19½")

3"(3½",4",4",4",4¾")

16"(17",19",21",23",24")

6"(6½",7",7½",8",9")

10"(10½",12",13½",15",15")

13½"(14¼",15¾",16",17",18")

Willow

Even a tomboy needs a hint of femininity in her wardrobe. This comfortably fitted tunic gets its shape from a ribbed bodice, while the non-ribbed tunic falls gracefully to just below hip length. Fitted sleeves in the same ribbing as the bodice keep the look neat and tidy through all kinds of adventures.

Measurements

Size	4	6	8	10	12	14
Child's Chest	23"	25"	27"	28"	30"	32"
Finished Sweater:						
Chest	24"	26½"	27½"	29"	31¼"	33½"
Cross Back (shoulder to shoulder)	9½"	11"	11¼"	11½"	12"	13¼"
Center Back Neck to Cuff	20½"	21½"	22¾"	25"	27"	28¼"

Materials

Yarn

660 (770, 890, 1020, 1180, 1370) yards worsted weight. Model is shown in Tatamy Tweed Worsted, by Kraemer Yarns, 4 (5, 5, 6, 7, 8) balls, Sea Blue Tweed.

Needles

24" circular needle, US size 7 (4.5 mm), or size needed to obtain gauge; 24" and 16" circular needles one size smaller for hem, sleeve cuffs, and neck trim

Other

Stitch markers, stitch holders, tapestry needle

Gauge

20 sts and 24 rows = 4" in stockinet stitch

Notes

1) Please read the Notes, Techniques, and Abbreviations section, p. 120, before you begin.

2) Sweater body is worked in the round from hem to underarms, then divided to work back and front separately. Sleeves are worked flat, separately, then sewn to body and seamed. Neckband and trim at hem are knitted on last.

3) To provide neat edges for finishing, when maintaining established ribbing pattern in shaped sections (armholes, front neck, and sleeve increases), it is best not to allow a lone purl stitch (RS) to sit on the edge. Knit these purl sts on the RS (purl them on the WS) until the shaping results in 2 knit sts on the outside edge; then resume established pattern.

Pattern Stitches

Ribbing pattern (in the round)

k1, *p1, k2, rep from * ending last repeat with k1

Ribbing pattern (for sleeves)

Row 1 (WS) *p2, k1, rep from * across, ending p2
Row 2 (RS) *k2, p1, rep from * across, ending k2

Instructions

Cast on at hem: With larger needle, CO 160 (176, 184, 192, 208, 224) sts. Join in a round, PM, and purl one round.

Tunic: Continue in stockinet stitch until sweater measures 10" (11½", 12", 13", 14", 14") from cast-on edge.

Begin bodice ribbing: Work a decrease round, as follows: k1, *p2tog, k2, rep from * ending last repeat with k1. There will be 120 (132, 138, 144, 156, 168) sts. Work even in ribbing pattern for 2".

Divide for back and front: Work across 57 (63, 66, 68, 74, 79) sts; BO 6 (6, 6, 8, 8, 10); work across 53 (59, 62, 63, 69, 73) sts; BO 6 (6, 6, 8, 8, 10). There will be 54 (60, 63, 64, 70, 74) sts for the back and 54 (60, 63, 64, 70, 74) sts for the front. Back and front are worked separately, flat, with RS rows in k2/p1 ribbing (in established pattern) and WS rows in p2/k1 ribbing (in established pattern). (See note 3, p. 44.)

Back: Work across sts for back in established pattern. Turn. Continue in established pattern, decreasing 1 st each side, every RS row, 3 (2, 3, 3, 4, 4) times, as follows: ssk, work to last 2 sts, k2tog. Continue in established pattern on 48 (56, 57, 58, 62, 66) sts until back measures 5" (5½", 6", 6½", 7", 8") above underarm bind-off sts, ending ready to work a RS row. BO 10 (14, 14, 14, 15, 17) sts for right shoulder. Work across 27 (27, 28, 29, 29, 31) sts. BO 10 (14, 14, 14, 15, 17) sts for left shoulder. Place 28 (28, 29, 30, 32, 32) sts at center on a stitch holder for back neck.

Front: From the WS, work across sts for front in established pattern. Turn. Continue in established pattern, decreasing 1 st each side, every RS row, 3 (2, 3, 3, 4, 4) times, as follows: ssk, work to last 2 sts, k2tog. Continue in established

(14, 15, 16, 18, 18) sts and place them on a stitch holder for center front. Work to end (17 [21, 21, 21, 22, 24]) sts for right shoulder.

Right shoulder: Continue with just the stitches for the right shoulder, decreasing 1 st at neck edge every RS row 7 times, as follows: ssk, work to end. Work even, as necessary, on 10 (14, 14, 14, 15, 17) sts to match back. BO in pattern.

Left shoulder: Begin at neck edge with a WS row and continue, decreasing 1 st at neck edge every RS row 7 times, as follows: work to last 2 sts, k2tog. Work even, as necessary, on 10 (14, 14, 14, 15, 17) sts to match right front and back. BO in pattern.

pattern on 48 (56, 57, 58, 62, 66) sts until front measures 2½" (2¾", 3", 3½", 4", 5") above underarm bind-off, ending ready to work a RS row. Work across the first 17 (21, 21, 21, 22, 24) sts and leave them on the right-hand needle for the left shoulder. Work across the center 14

Sleeves: With smaller needle, CO 35 (38, 41, 44, 47, 47) sts. Beginning with a WS row (and working flat), work in ribbing pattern for sleeves for 9 rows. Switch to larger needle and continue in ribbing pattern for 18 (12, 10, 16, 16, 6) rows. Work an increase row on the next row and every 6th row thereafter 7 (8, 9, 10, 11, 7) times more, then every 4th row 0 (0, 0, 0, 0, 0, 9) times, as follows: kfb, work to last st, kfb, working new sts into established ribbing pattern (see note 3, p. 44). There will be 51 (56, 61, 66, 71, 81) sts. Continue working even as necessary until sleeve measures 12½" (12½", 13¼", 15", 16", 16¼") from cast-on edge, measured at center, ending ready to work a RS row. BO 4 (4, 4, 5, 5, 6) sts at the beginning of the next two rows. Decrease 1 st each side every RS row 3 (2, 3, 3, 4, 4) times, as follows: ssk, k to last 2 sts, k2tog. Decrease 1 st each side every row 7 (11, 11, 13, 13, 17) times, as follows: (RS rows) ssk, k to last 2 sts, k2tog; (WS rows) p2tog, p to last 2 sts, ssp. BO 2 (2, 3, 3, 4, 4) sts at the beginning of the next 4 rows. BO remaining 15 (14, 13, 12, 15, 11) sts. Repeat for second sleeve.

Weave in ends and block pieces. Join front to back at shoulders.

Add neckband: With smaller 16" needle, from the RS, beginning at left shoulder seam, pick up and knit sts between shoulder and center front stitch holder, adjusting as necessary to maintain the continuity of the established pattern across center back and center front (see also Techniques section, p. 121). Work across sts from stitch holder at center front in established pattern. Pick up and knit sts along right neck edge, adjusting as necessary to maintain the continuity of the established pattern across center front and center back. Work across sts from stitch holder at center back in established pattern. Work in established k2/p1 ribbing for 7 rounds. BO in pattern.

Add I-cord at hem: With smaller 24" needle, from the RS, beginning at a point below the left underarm, pick up and knit stitches along the cast-on (hem) edge (see Techniques section, p. 121). Work a 3-st attached I-cord around the hem edge. Join beginning to end with a short seam.

Finishing: Sew sleeves to armholes and sew long under-sleeve seams. Weave in ends and block edging if desired.

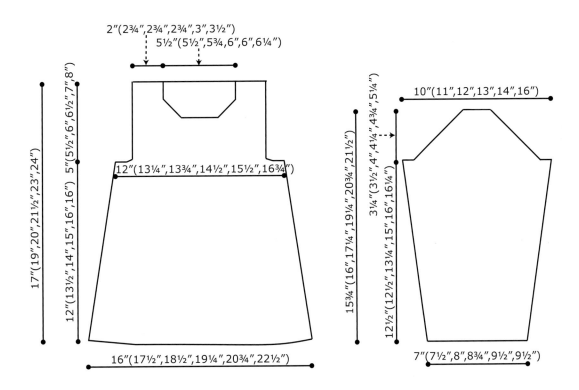

2"(2¾",2¾",2¾",3",3½")

5½"(5½",5¾",6",6",6¼")

17"(19",20",21½",23",24")

12"(13½",14",15",16",16")

5"(5½",6",6½",7",8")

12"(13¼",13¾",14½",15½",16¾")

16"(17½",18½",19¼",20¾",22½")

10"(11",12",13",14",16")

15¾"(16",17¼",19¼",20¾",21½")

3¼"(3½",4",4¼",4¾",5¼")

12½"(12½",13¼",15",16",16¼")

7"(7½",8",8¾",9½",9½")

Beachcomber

Michigan is surrounded by some of the most beautiful beaches in the world. On the shores of Gitchigoomie (Lake Superior) in Michigan's Upper Peninsula, every day can be a sweater day, even in the height of summer. This ruggedly handsome, top-down, raglan sweater is just right for a day at Great Sand Bay. A textured rib pattern on the sleeves adds extra interest.

Measurements

Size	4	6	8	10	12	14
Child's Chest	23″	25″	27″	28″	30″	32″
Finished Sweater:						
Chest	28″	30″	32″	33″	35″	37″
Cross Back (shoulder to shoulder)	9¾″	10¼″	10¾″	11¼″	12″	12¼″
Center Back Neck to Cuff	21″	21¾″	22¾″	25″	27¼″	28″

Materials

Yarn

715 (830, 900, 1045, 1155, 1255) yards worsted weight. Model is shown in Perfection, by Kraemer Yarns, 4 (4, 4, 5, 6, 6) balls; color number Y1520, Quartz.

Needles

16″ and 24″ circular needles, US size 9 (5.5 mm), or size needed to obtain gauge; 16″ circular needle one size smaller for neckband

Other

Stitch markers, long stitch holders or waste yarn, tapestry needle

Gauge

20 sts and 26 rows = 4" in stockinet stitch
18 sts and 28 rows = 4" in pattern stitch

Notes

1) Please read the Notes, Techniques, and Abbreviations section, p. 120, before you begin.

2) Sweater body is worked with top-down sweater construction. The neck is knit flat until depth of neck at center front is achieved. Stitches are then cast on at center front, work is joined in a round, and the yoke is completed in the round. When armhole depth is achieved, sleeve stitches are placed on waste yarn, stitches are cast on at underarms, and the body of the sweater is worked in the round. Once the body is completed, each sleeve is knit down from the active sleeve sts, then seamed. Stitches are picked up at the neck, knitting the neckband on last.

Pattern Stitches

Only the sleeves are worked in a broken rib pattern, as follows:

Sleeves worked flat (in yoke)

Row 1 (WS) *k1, p1, rep from *, end k1
Row 2 (RS) knit
Row 3 *p1, k1, rep from *, end p1
Row 4 rep row 2

Sleeves worked in the round (in yoke)

Round 1 (RS) ribbed in established pattern
Round 2 (RS) knit

Sleeves worked flat (below yoke)

Row 1 (WS) purl
Row 2 (RS) ribbed in established pattern

Whisper Ribbing (at sweater hem, see also Techniques, p. 121)

On what would be the first round of ribbing, instead of purling every other stitch, purl only every 4th stitch around (a 3 x 1 ribbing). On the next round, begin 1 x 1 ribbing. Don't be concerned on the first round if the numbers don't work out exactly evenly, since not every sweater will have a stitch count divisible by 4. Just make sure that you only purl a stitch that will continue to be purled on subsequent rounds of ribbing.

Instructions

Cast on at neck: With larger 16" needle, CO 1, PM (right front), CO 1, PM (decorative seam stitch), CO 7 (7, 7, 7, 7, 9), PM (right sleeve), CO 1, PM (decorative seam stitch), CO 21 (25, 29, 29, 27, 31), PM (back), CO 1, PM (decorative seam stitch), CO 7 (7, 7, 7, 7, 9), PM (left sleeve), CO 1, PM (decorative seam stitch), CO 1 (left front).

There will be a total of 41 (45, 49, 49, 47, 55) sts.

Note: Front and back sections, and seam sts, are worked in stockinet stitch. Sleeve sections are worked in broken rib.

Continue working neckline flat
First row: (WS) Purl front and back sections and seam sts and work across sleeve sections in broken rib.

Second row: (RS) kfb, k to marker, *M1R, sl m, k1, sl m, M1L, k to marker, rep from * across, ending with M1R, sl m, k1, sl m, M1L, k to last st, kfb.

Note: The next WS row will have 2 more sts in each section. Incorporate all new sts by working in the established broken rib pattern for each section.

Continue alternating these two rows, increasing by 10 sts on each RS row until there are 111 (115, 119, 119, 117, 125) sts, distributed as follows: 15 sts in right front, 1 st (seam), 21 (21, 21, 21, 21, 23) sts in right sleeve, 1 st (seam), 35 (39, 43, 43, 41, 45) sts in back, 1 st (seam), 21 (21, 21, 21, 21, 23) sts in left sleeve, 1 st (seam), and 15 sts in left front.

Note: End with a RS row.

Join neck and continue yoke in the round: Turn the work and use a cable cast-on to CO 5 (9, 13, 13, 11, 15) sts (center front) at the end of the previous row. Turn. Join in a round and knit to the first marker. This is now the end of round marker.

Round 1: Work in established pattern, remembering to rib across the sleeve sections in established pattern.
Round 2: *sl m, k1, sl m, M1L, k to marker, M1R, rep from * around.

Continue increasing every second round 9 (6, 5, 7, 11, 10) times and then every fourth round 4 (6, 7, 7, 6, 8) times, switching to 24″ needle, if desired.

There will be 220 (220, 228, 244, 264, 284) sts, distributed as follows: 1 st (seam), 47 (45, 45, 49, 55, 59) sts in right sleeve, 1 st (seam), 61 (63, 67, 71, 75, 81) sts in back, 1 st (seam), 47 (45, 45, 49, 55, 59) sts in left sleeve, 1 st (seam), and 61 (63, 67, 71, 75, 81) sts in front.

Put sleeve sts on hold and work body in the round: Removing markers as you work the next round, knit 1 (decorative seam stitch), place the next 47 (45, 45, 49, 55, 59) sts on a long stitch holder or waste yarn (right sleeve). Turn work and use a cable cast-on to CO 7 (10, 11, 9, 10, 9) sts. Turn and resume knitting to next sleeve (knitting decorative seam stitches). Place the next 47 (45, 45, 49, 55, 59) sts on a long stitch holder or waste yarn (left sleeve). Turn work. Use a cable cast-on to CO 7 (10, 11, 9, 10, 9) sts. Turn and resume knitting to end of round. Place end of round marker.

Work even in stockinet stitch on 140 (150, 160, 164, 174, 184) sts until sweater measures 9¼″ (11″, 11″, 13″, 13½″, 13″) below underarm.

Work 1 round of whisper ribbing. Continue in 1 x 1 ribbing for 5 rounds. BO loosely in ribbing.

Work sleeves flat: Place 47 (45, 45, 49, 55, 59) sts for first sleeve back on the needle. Use a cable cast-on to CO 4 (5, 6, 5, 6, 5) sts at the beginning of the row (RS). Work across, working new sts into established ribbing pattern. Turn. Use a cable cast-on to CO 4 (5, 6, 5, 6, 5) sts at the end of the row. There will be 55 (55, 57, 59, 67, 69) sts. Purl this, and all WS rows, even. (All RS rows will be worked in established ribbing pattern.)

On the next row (RS), and every 6th row thereafter, 10 (9, 10, 10, 14, 13) times more (for a total of 11 [10, 11, 11, 15, 14] times), work a decrease row as follows: ssk, work in established ribbing pattern to last 2 sts, k2tog.

There will be 33 (35, 35, 37, 37, 41) sts remaining after the last decrease row. Continue working even, as necessary, until sleeve, from underarm, measures 10¼" (10½", 11", 12½", 14¼", 14"). Work in 1 x 1 ribbing for 12 rows, following from established pattern. BO loosely in ribbing.

Repeat for second sleeve.

Add neckband: Beginning to the left of the seam at the visual right of the center section (left shoulder), from the RS, with smaller 16" needle, pick up and knit an odd number of sts along front of neck (see Techniques section, p. 121). Pick up and knit 1 st in the seam st. Pick up and knit 7 (7, 7, 7, 7, 9) sts across the top of the right sleeve. Pick up and knit 1 st in the seam st. Pick up and knit 21 (25, 29, 29, 27, 31) sts across back of neck. Pick up and knit 1 st in the seam st. Pick up and knit 7 (7, 7, 7, 7, 9) sts across the top of the left sleeve. Pick up and knit 1 st in the last seam st. Join in a round and PM. Work a 1 x 1 ribbed neckband, beginning with a purl st, for 6 rounds. BO loosely in ribbing.

Finishing: Sew seams from cuffs to underarms for each sleeve. Join sleeves to sweater with short seams at underarms.

Weave in ends and block.

Back: Work flat in established pattern until armhole measures 6″ (6½″, 7″, 7½″, 8″, 9″) above underarm bind-off row, ending ready to work a RS row. BO 16 (18, 18, 20, 22, 23) sts in pattern. Work across the next 28 (28, 32, 32, 32, 34) sts and place 29 (29, 33, 33, 33, 35) sts on a stitch holder for center back. BO to end in pattern.

Front: Beginning at the right underarm, work a WS row across sts for front. Continue working flat in established pattern until front of sweater measures 15″ (16½″, 18″, 20″, 21″, 23″) from cast-on edge, ending ready to work a RS row. Work across the first 22 (24, 26, 28, 30, 31) sts and leave them on the right-hand needle for the left shoulder. Work across the center 17 (17, 17, 17, 17, 19) sts and place them on a stitch holder for center front. Work to end (right shoulder).

Right shoulder: Continue with just the stitches for the right shoulder, decreasing 1 st at neck edge every RS row 6 (6, 8, 8, 8, 8) times, as follows: ssk, work to end. Work even, as necessary, on 16 (18,

18, 20, 22, 23) sts until armhole measures 6" (6½", 7", 7½", 8", 9") above underarm bind-off row, to match back. BO in pattern.

Left shoulder: Begin at neck edge with a WS row and continue, decreasing 1 st at neck edge every RS row 6 (6, 8, 8, 8, 8) times, as follows: work to last 2 sts, k2tog. Work even, as necessary, on 16 (18, 18, 20, 22, 23) sts until armhole measures 6" (6½", 7", 7½", 8", 9") above underarm bind-off row, to match right front and back. BO in pattern.

Sew fronts to back at shoulders.

Sleeves: From the right side, with larger needle, leaving underarm bound-off stitches free, pick up and knit 63 (67, 75, 79, 83, 95) sts along armhole edge. Beginning with a WS row, work in p3/k1 ribbing across, ending p3. Continue in established pattern, decreasing 1 st each side every 6th row 9 (10, 9, 9, 10, 4) times, then every 4th row 5 (4, 7, 9, 10, 20) times, as follows: ssk, work to end, k2tog. *At the same time*, when the sleeve measures 11" (11½", 12¼", 13¾", 15½", 16"), work 3 rows in CC1, followed by 2 rows in CC2, followed by 5 rows in CC1. Work 9 rows more in MC, completing decreases. The last row is worked in k1/p1 ribbing, matching purl sts with existing purl sts. BO remaining 35 (39, 43, 43, 43, 47) sts.

Sew one-half of the bound-off underarm sts to the top front edge of the sleeve. Sew the other half of the bound-off underarm sts to the top back edge of the sleeve. Sew long under-sleeve seam. Repeat for second sleeve.

Add neckband: With MC and smaller needle, beginning at left shoulder, from the RS, pick up and knit sts along left neck edge, adjusting as necessary to maintain the continuity of the established pattern across center back and center front (see Techniques section, p. 121). Work across sts from stitch holder at center front. Pick up and knit sts along right neck edge, adjusting as necessary to maintain the continuity of the established pattern across center front and center back. Work across sts from stitch holder at center back. Work in established k3/p1 ribbing for 2" (2½", 2½", 2½", 3", 3"). BO in pattern.

Finishing: Weave in ends and block.

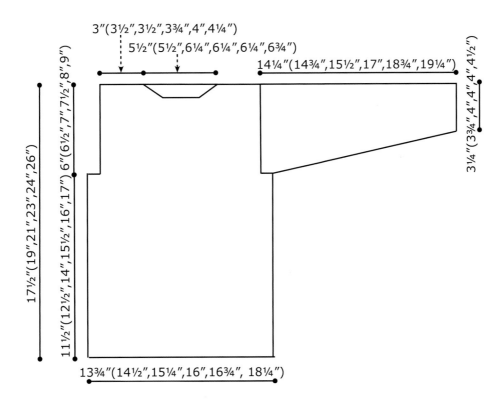

3"(3½",3½",3¾",4",4¼")

5½"(5½",6¼",6¼",6¼",6¾")

14¼"(14¾",15½",17",18¾",19¼")

3¼"(3¾",4",4",4",4½")

17½"(19",21",23",24",26")

11½"(12½",14",15½",16",17") 6"(6½",7",7½",8",9")

13¾"(14½",15¼",16",16¾", 18¼")

Even the oldest jeans and play-day flannel shirt can benefit from just a little dressing up. A subtle texture makes this wardrobe basic a bit more fun, but still quiet enough to meet with his approval.

Measurements

Size	4	6	8	10	12	14
Child's Chest	23"	25"	27"	28"	30"	32"
Finished Sweater:						
Chest	28½"	30"	32"	33½"	35"	37"
Cross Back (shoulder to shoulder)	10½"	11½"	11½"	12"	13"	13¼"

Materials

Yarn

360 (400, 475, 550, 600, 700) yards worsted weight. Model is shown in Encore Worsted, by Plymouth Yarn, 2 (2, 3, 3, 3, 4) balls; color number 194, Gray Frost.

Needles

24" circular needle, US size 7 (4.5mm), or size needed to obtain gauge; 16" circular needle one size smaller for neck and armhole trim

Other

Stitch markers, stitch holders, tapestry needle

Gauge

19 sts and 26 rows = 4" in pattern stitch

Notes

1) Please read the Notes, Techniques, and Abbreviations section, p. 120, before you begin.

2) Vest is worked in the round from hem to underarms, then divided to work back and front separately. Ribbed trim at neck and armholes is knitted on last.

Pattern Stitches

Ribbing (worked in the round)

Round 1 *k3, p1, rep from * around
Rep this round for ribbing.

Overall pattern stitch (worked in the round from hem to underarms)

Round 1 k1, *sl1 wyif, k3, rep from * around, end k2
Rounds 2-4 knit
Round 5 *k3, sl1 wyif, rep from * around
Rounds 6-8 knit
Rep rounds 1-8 for pattern.

Overall pattern stitch (worked flat above underarm bind-off round)

Row 1 k1, *sl1 wyif, k3, rep from * across, end k2
Row 2 purl
Row 3 knit
Row 4 purl
Row 5 *k3, sl1 wyif, rep from * across
Row 6 purl
Row 7 knit
Row 8 purl
Rep rows 1-8 for pattern.

Instructions

Cast on at hem: With larger needle, CO 136 (144, 152, 160, 168, 176) sts. Join in a round, PM, and work in ribbing pattern for 5 rounds. Begin with round 7 of overall pattern stitch and work in pattern stitch until vest measures 9½" (10", 11½", 13", 13½", 13½"); then continue working in established pattern until you can end ready to work round 2 or round 6 of pattern.

Divide for back and fronts: k64 (67, 70, 74, 78, 82) sts; BO 8 (10, 12, 12, 12, 12) sts;

k59 (61, 63, 67, 71, 75) sts; BO 8 (10, 12, 12, 12, 12) sts. There will be 60 (62, 64, 68, 72, 76) sts for the vest back and 60 (62, 64, 68, 72, 76) sts for the vest front.

Back: Knit across sts for back. Purl one row. Work the back sts in established pattern, decreasing 1 st at each side, every RS row, 5 (4, 5, 5, 5, 6) times, as follows: ssk, work to last 2 sts, k2tog. Work even in established pattern until armholes measure 7½″ (8″, 8½″, 9″, 9½″, 10½″) above underarm bind-off round, ending ready to work a RS row. Work across 12 (14, 13, 15, 17, 17) sts for right

Molly

shoulder and place them on a stitch holder. BO center 26 (26, 28, 28, 28, 30) sts for back neck. Work to end, placing 12 (14, 13, 15, 17, 17) sts for left shoulder on a stitch holder.

Front: From the RS, beginning at left underarm, knit across sts for front. Purl one row. Continue in established pattern, as for back, decreasing 1 st at each side, every RS row, 5 (4, 5, 5, 5, 6) times, *except*, when front measures 1½″ above underarm bind-off round, ending ready to work a RS row, divide front. Work right and left sides separately, as follows: Work to center, turn, work back, maintaining established pattern and completing required decreases at underarm edge.

Left front: Decrease 1 st at neck edge, each RS row, 7 (6, 7, 5, 3, 2) times, as follows: work to last 2 sts, k2tog. Then, decrease 1 st at neck edge, every other RS row, 6 (7, 7, 9, 11, 13) times. Continue working in established pattern on 12 (14, 13, 15, 17, 17) sts as necessary, until armhole measures 7½″ (8″, 8½″, 9″, 9½″,

10½") above underarm bind-off round, to match back. Place shoulder sts on a stitch holder.

Right front: (Begin at center front.) Work across sts for right front and work back, maintaining established pattern and completing required decreases at underarm edge. Decrease 1 st at neck edge, each RS row, 7 (6, 7, 5, 3, 2) times, as follows: ssk, work to end. Then decrease 1 st at neck edge, every other RS row, 6 (7, 7, 9, 11, 13) times. Continue working in established pattern on 12 (14, 13, 15, 17, 17) sts as necessary, until armhole measures 7½" (8", 8½", 9", 9½", 10½") above underarm bind-off round, to match back. Place shoulder sts on a stitch holder.

Join shoulders with the three-needle bind-off technique.

Add armhole trim: Beginning at center of underarm bind-off, from the RS, with 16" needle, pick up and knit sts around the armhole, as follows: pick up and knit 1 st for each st in underarm bind-off, 3 sts of each 4 rows along shaped area, and 4 sts of each 5 rows along straight edges, decreasing to 3 sts of each 4 rows for several inches either side of shoulder seam. Adjust sts to a multiple of 4. Join in a round, PM, and work in ribbing pattern for 5 rounds. BO loosely in ribbing pattern. Repeat for second armhole.

Add neck trim: Beginning at center front, from the RS, with 16" needle, pick up and knit sts around the neck: pick up and knit 4 sts for every 5 rows along front edges and 1 st for each st across back neck edge. Adjust sts to a multiple of 4 plus 3. Join in a round, PM, and work one round of ribbing pattern, beginning and ending with k3.

Round 2: k2tog, continue in established ribbing pattern to last 2 sts, ssk.

Round 3: work even in established ribbing pattern.

Round 4: rep round 2.

Round 5: rep round 3.

BO loosely in ribbing pattern, working the first two sts and the last two sts as for rounds 2 and 4.

Finishing: Weave in ends and block.

2½"(3",2¾",3",3½",3½")

5½"(5½",6",6",6",6¼")

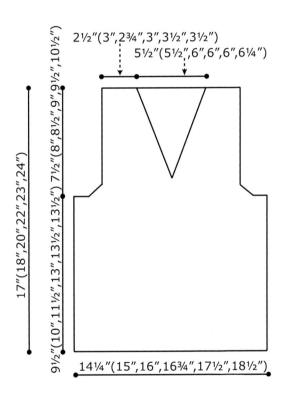

17"(18",20",22",23",24")

9½"(10",11½",13",13½",13½") 7½"(8",8½",9",9½",10½")

14¼"(15",16",16¾",17½",18½")

armhole measures 5″ (5½″, 6″, 6½″, 7″, 8″) above underarm bind-off row (to match back and right shoulder), ending ready to work row 3 or row 7. Place sts on a stitch holder for left shoulder.

Sleeves: Sleeves are worked flat, as separate pieces, from cuff to armhole edge. With smaller needle, CO 37 (37, 43, 43, 43, 49) sts. Work 5 rows of ribbing pattern for cuffs. Switch to larger needle and begin overall pattern stitch with row 5 and work in overall pattern stitch through row 4. Work an increase row on the next row and every 8th (8th, 8th, 8th, 6th, 6th) row thereafter 7 (9, 9, 11, 14, 16) times more, as follows: k2, M1R, work to last 2 sts in established pattern, M1L, k2. Work new sts into established pattern as soon as there are 2 edge sts before the first wkeye. There will be 53 (57, 63, 67, 73, 83) sts following the last increase. Continue in established pattern until sleeve measures 14½″ (15½″, 16″, 18″, 19¼″, 20¼″) when measured at center, ending ready to work row 3 or 7. BO. Repeat for second sleeve.

Join front to back with a three-needle bind-off at shoulders. Sew top of sleeve to armhole edge. Sew one-half of the bound-off underarm sts to the top front edge of the sleeve. Sew the other half of the bound-off underarm sts to the top back edge of the sleeve. Sew long under-sleeve seam. Repeat for second sleeve.

Add neckband: From the RS, beginning at left shoulder seam, with smaller 16" needle, pick up and knit sts around the neck edge (see Techniques section, p. 121). Knit 8 rounds. Using larger needle, BO loosely.

Finishing: Weave in ends and block.

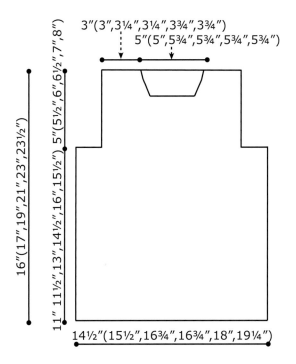

3"(3",3¼",3¼",3¾",3¾")

5"(5",5¾",5¾",5¾",5¾")

16"(17",19",21",23",23½")

11" 11½",13",14½",16",15½") 5"(5½",6",6½",7",8")

14½"(15½",16¾",16¾",18",19¼")

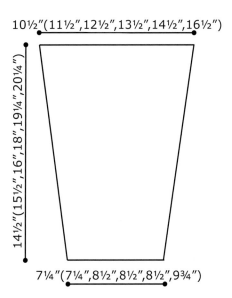

10½"(11½",12½",13½",14½",16½")

14½"(15½",16",18",19¼",20¼")

7¼"(7¼",8½",8½",8½",9¾")

Head of the Class

When I was in grade school, my sisters and I had school cardigans. They were white (so they would "go" with all our dresses). We took them to school on Mondays and brought them home for laundering on Fridays. I don't know how my mother ever got those white sleeves clean. Here is my own version of a school cardigan to make in any color (except white!) with fitted sleeves and a dainty edging I call "string of pearls."

Measurements

Size	4	6	8	10	12	14
Child's Chest	23"	25"	27"	28"	30"	32"
Finished Sweater:						
Chest	26½"	28"	30½"	31"	33"	35"
Cross Back (shoulder to shoulder)	9¼"	10½"	11"	11"	11½"	13"
Center Back Neck to Cuff	19½"	20½"	22"	24"	26"	27¾"

Materials

Yarn

550 (625, 750, 875, 1020, 1150) yards worsted weight. Model is shown in 220 Superwash, by Cascade Yarns, 3 (3, 4, 4, 5, 6) balls; color number 1922.

Needles

24" circular needle, US size 7 (4.5 mm), or size needed to obtain gauge; double-point or straight needle, one size smaller for "string of pearls" edging

Other

Stitch holders, tapestry needle, and 5 (5, 6, 7, 7, 8) ⅝″ buttons

Gauge

20 sts and 28 rows = 4″ in stockinet stitch

Notes

1) Please read the Notes, Techniques, and Abbreviations section, p. 120, before you begin.

2) Sweater body is worked flat, as one piece, from hem to underarms, then divided to work back and fronts separately. Sleeves are worked flat, separately, then sewn to body and seamed. Stitches are picked up along center fronts to work button bands. Stitches are picked up at neck to knit the neck trim last.

Pattern stitches

Ribbing (at hem)

Row 1 (WS) p3, *k2, p2, rep from *, end p3 (instead of p2)
Row 2 (RS) k3, *p2, k2, rep from *, end k3 (instead of k2)
Rep these 2 rows for ribbing at hem.

Ribbing (at cuffs)

Row 1 (WS) *p2, k2, rep from *, end p2
Row 2 (RS) *k2, p2, rep from *, end k2
Rep these 2 rows for ribbing at cuffs.

Whisper Ribbing (see also, Techniques, p. 121)

On the last row of ribbing (RS), instead of purling two stitches between each two knitted stitches, purl just one, as follows: (at the hem) k4, *p1, k3, rep from * across; and (at the cuffs) k3, *p1, k3, rep from * across.

String of Pearls edging

The edging is worked from the WS with a needle one size smaller than that used for the body, as follows:

k2, BO 1, *knit in the front/the back/the front/the back/and the front again of the next stitch, pull the first 4 loops from this group over the 5th loop, BO over remaining loop, k1 tbl, BO 1, k1, BO 1, rep from * across.

Instructions

Cast on at hem: With circular needle, CO 132 (140, 152, 156, 164, 176) sts. Work in ribbing for hem for 7 rows. Work 1 row of whisper ribbing. Beginning with a WS row, work even in stockinet stitch until sweater measures 11" (11½", 13", 14½", 16", 15½") from cast-on, ending ready to work a RS row.

Divide back and fronts: On the next row, k28 (30, 33, 33, 35, 38). Keeping those sts on the right-hand needle for the right front, BO 10 (10, 10, 12, 12, 12) sts. Knit to end. On the next row, p28 (30,

33, 33, 35, 38). Keeping those sts on the right-hand needle for the left front, BO 10 (10, 10, 12, 12, 12) sts. There will be 56 (60, 66, 66, 70, 76) sts for the back, and 28 (30, 33, 33, 35, 38) sts for each front section.

Back: Purl across sts for back. Decrease 1 st each side, every RS row 5 (4, 5, 5, 6, 6) times, as follows: k1, ssk, k to last 3 sts, k2tog, k1. Work even on remaining 46 (52, 56, 56, 58, 64) sts until armhole depth (above bind-off row) is 5" (5½", 6", 6½", 7", 8"), ending ready to work a RS row. Knit across 10 (12, 13, 14, 15, 17) sts for right shoulder and place them on a stitch holder. BO the center 26 (28, 30, 28, 28, 30) sts. Knit to end, placing the remaining 10 (12, 13, 14, 15, 17) sts on a stitch holder for left shoulder.

Right front: Beginning at underarm with a WS row, purl across the sts for right front. Turn. Decrease 1 st at underarm edge every RS row 5 (4, 5, 5, 6, 6) times, as follows: k to last 3 sts, k2tog, k1. Work even on 23 (26, 28, 28, 29, 32) sts until armhole measures 2½" (2¾", 3", 3½", 4",

5″), ending ready to work a RS row. BO 7 (8, 9, 8, 8, 9) sts and knit to end. Decrease 1 st at neck edge every RS row 6 times, as follows: k1, ssk, k to end. Work even on 10 (12, 13, 14, 15, 17) sts until armhole measures 5″ (5½″, 6″, 6½″, 7″, 8″), to match back. Place sts on a stitch holder for right shoulder.

Left front: Beginning at underarm with a RS row, work a decrease at underarm edge on this and every RS row 4 (3, 4, 4, 5, 5) times more as follows: k1, ssk, k to end. Work even on 23 (26, 28, 28, 29, 32) sts until armhole measures 2½″ (2¾″, 3″, 3½″, 4″, 5″), ending ready to work a WS row. BO 7 (8, 9, 8, 8, 9) sts and purl to end. Decrease 1 st at neck edge every RS row 6 times, as follows: k to last 3 sts, k2tog, k1. Work even on 10 (12, 13, 14, 15, 17) sts until armhole measures 5″ (5½″, 6″, 6½″, 7″, 8″), to match back and right front. Place sts on a stitch holder for left shoulder.

Sleeves: CO 38 (38, 42, 42, 46, 46) sts. Work in ribbing for cuff for 11 rows. Work 1 row of whisper ribbing. Continue in stockinet stitch, increasing 1 st each side every 10th (6th, 6th, 6th, 6th, 6th) row 6 (9, 9, 12, 12, 12) times, then every 4th row 0 (0, 0, 0, 0, 5) times as follows: k1, kfb, k to last 3 sts, kfb, k2. Continue in stockinet stitch on 50 (56, 60, 66, 70, 80) sts as necessary until sleeve measures 11¾″ (11¾″, 12½″, 14½″, 15¾″, 16¼″) from cuff, measured at center, ending ready to work a RS row. BO 6 (6, 6, 7, 7, 7) sts at the beginning of the next two rows. Decrease 1 st each side every RS row 5 (4, 5, 5, 6, 7) times, as follows: k1, ssk, k to last 3 sts, k2tog, k1. Purl one row. Decrease 1 st each side every row 6 (10, 11, 12, 13, 15) times, as follows: (RS rows) ssk, k to last 2 sts, k2tog; (WS rows) p2tog, p to last 2 sts, ssp. BO 2 sts at the beginning of the next 4 rows. BO remaining 8 (8, 8, 10, 10, 14) sts. Repeat for second sleeve.

Weave in ends and block pieces. Join fronts to back with a three-needle bind-off at shoulders.

Add button bands

Right front: From the RS, beginning at hem, pick up and knit sts along center edge of right front (see Techniques section, p. 121). Place markers on the needle for 5 (5, 6, 7, 7, 8) buttonholes.

An easy way to do this is to first place a marker about 4 sts up from the hem edge and a second marker about 4 sts down from the neck edge. Now, count

the number of sts between these markers. Divide these sts by the number of buttons less 1. If the number of sts does not divide evenly, adjust the number between the top and bottom markers by adding to the center st count, by subtracting from the top or bottom, or by adding one or more stitches to the top or bottom from the center. Once the sts in the center can be evenly divided, place the remaining markers at evenly spaced intervals.

Turn. Purl one row. Make buttonholes on the next row as follows: *k to marker, yo (removing marker), k2tog, rep from *, knitting to the end of the row. Work 2 more rows in stockinet stitch. On the next row, bind off with the String of Pearls edging.

Left front: From the RS, beginning at neck edge, pick up and knit sts along center edge of left front (see Techniques section, p. 121). Work in stockinet stitch for 4 rows. Bind off with the String of Pearls edging, as for right front band.

Add neck edging: Beginning at right front neck edge of buttonhole band, pick up and knit sts around the neck (see Techniques section, p. 121). Bind off with the String of Pearls edging, as for button bands.

Finishing: Sew sleeves to armholes. Sew under-sleeve seams, from armhole to cuff. Weave in ends. Steam seams and edging. Sew buttons to left front button band, opposite buttonholes in right front band.

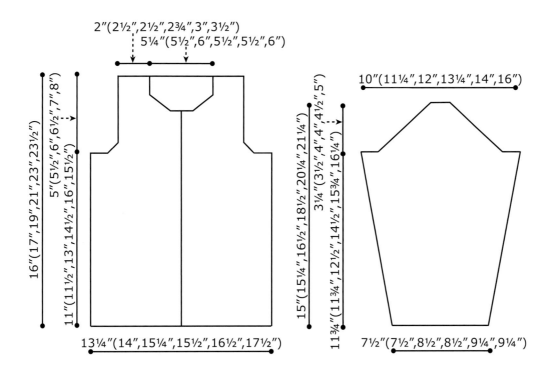

2"(2½",2½",2¾",3",3½")

5¼"(5½",6",5½",5½",6")

16"(17",19",21",23",23½")

5"(5½",6",6½",7",8")

11"(11½",13",14½",16",15½")

13¼"(14",15¼",15½",16½",17½")

15"(15¼",16½",18½",20¼",21¼")

3¼"(3½",4",4",4½",5")

11¾"(11¾",12½",14½",15¾",16¼")

10"(11¼",12",13¼",14",16")

7½"(7½",8½",8½",9¼",9¼")

This charming vest gets its tickle from lace ribbing extending from the top of the ribcage to the hem. My version is a go-with-anything color, but, made in a favorite color, it will tickle any girl's fancy.

Measurements

Size	4	6	8	10	12	14
Child's Chest	23″	25″	27″	28″	30″	32″
Finished Sweater:						
Chest	26½″	28″	29½″	31″	32½″	35″
Cross Back (shoulder to shoulder)	9¾″	10½″	10½″	11½″	11½″	12¼″

Materials

Yarn

245 (280, 345, 400, 445, 500) yards worsted weight. Model is shown in Greenland, by Cascade Yarns, 2 (3, 3, 3, 4, 4) balls, color number 3500.

Needles

24″ circular needle, US size 9 (5.5 mm), or size needed to obtain gauge; 16″ circular needle one size smaller for neck and armhole trim

Other

Stitch marker, stitch holders, tapestry needle

Gauge

19 sts and 24 rows = 4″ in stockinet stitch

Notes

1) Please read the Notes, Techniques, and Abbreviations section, p. 120, before you begin.

2) Vest body is worked in the round from the hem to the armhole bind-off. Back and front are then worked separately, flat. Neck and armhole edging are knitted on last.

Pattern Stitches

Eyelet ribbing

Round 1: p1, *k2tog, yo, k1, yo, ssk, p2, rep from * around, ending last rep with p1
Rounds 2-4: p1, *k5, p2, rep from * around, ending last rep with p1
Rep these four rounds for eyelet ribbing pattern.

Instructions

Cast on at hem: With larger needle, CO 126 (133, 140, 147, 154, 168) sts. Join in a round, PM, and work rounds 1-4 of eyelet ribbing pattern until body measures 4½″ (5″, 6½″, 7½″, 8″, 8″) from cast-on edge, ending with round 1. Continue in stockinet stitch until body measures 6½″ (7″, 8½″, 9½″, 10″, 10″).

Divide back and fronts: Knit 58 (62, 63, 68, 71, 76); BO 10 (10, 14, 10, 12, 16); k52 (55, 55, 63, 64, 67); BO 10 (10, 14, 10, 12, 16). There will be 53 (57, 56, 63, 65, 68) sts for the back and 53 (56, 56, 64, 65, 68) sts for the front.

Back: Work across sts for back (RS). Turn. Purl one row. Continue in stockinet stitch, decreasing 1 st each side, every RS row 3 (3, 3, 4, 4, 4) times, as follows: ssk, k to last 2 sts, k2tog. Continue working even on 47 (51, 50, 55, 57, 60) sts, until armhole measures 5″ (5½″, 6″, 6½″, 7″, 8″) above underarm bind-off row, ending ready to work a RS row. Knit across the first 11 (12, 12, 14, 15, 16) sts and place them on a stitch holder for right shoulder. BO the center 25 (27, 26, 27, 27, 28) sts. Knit to end, placing the remaining 11 (12, 12, 14, 15, 16) sts on a stitch holder for left shoulder.

Front: Beginning with a RS row, work as for back through armhole decreases. Continue working even on 47 (50, 50, 56, 57, 60) sts, until armhole measures 2½″ (3″, 3″, 3½″, 4″, 4½″) above underarm bind-off row, ending ready to work a RS row. Knit 14 (15, 15, 17, 18, 19) sts. BO the next 19 (20, 20, 22, 21, 22) sts. Knit to end.

Right shoulder: Turn. Purl across sts for right shoulder. Continue in stockinet stitch, decreasing 1 st at neck edge every RS row 3 times, as follows: ssk, k to end. Work even on 11 (12, 12, 14, 15, 16) sts until armhole measures 5″ (5½″, 6″, 6½″, 7″, 8″) above underarm bind-off row, to

match back. Place sts for right shoulder on a stitch holder.

Left shoulder: Beginning with a WS row, purl. Continue in stockinet stitch, decreasing 1 st at neck edge every RS row 3 times, as follows: k to last 2 sts, k2tog. Work even on 11 (12, 12, 14, 15, 16) sts to match right shoulder. Place sts for left shoulder on a stitch holder.

Join back and front at shoulders using the three-needle bind-off technique.

Add armhole trim: With smaller needle, from the RS, pick up and knit 3 sts for every 4 sts and 3 sts for every 4 rows around one armhole. Purl one round. BO as follows: *p2tog, place remaining st back on left-hand needle, rep from * around. Repeat for second armhole.

Add neck trim: With smaller needle, from the RS, pick up and knit 3 sts for every 4 sts and 3 sts for every 4 rows around neck edge. Complete as for armholes.

Finishing: Weave in·ends and block.

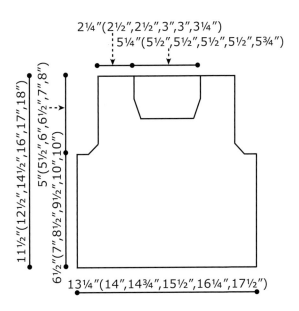

2¼"(2½",2½",3",3",3¼")

5¼"(5½",5½",5½",5½",5¾")

11½"(12½",14½",16",17",18")

5"(5½",6",6½",7",8")

6½"(7",8½",9½",10",10")

13¼"(14",14¾",15½",16¼",17½")

The inspiration for this sweater came from one of my favorite movies, "My Dog Skip." The main character might have worn a sweater like this to school in the 1940s. Subtle edging design, modified dropped shoulders, and a V-neck make it a timeless choice for a boy's school cardigan today.

Measurements

Size	4	6	8	10	12	14
Child's Chest	23"	25"	27"	28"	30"	32"
Finished Sweater:						
Chest	27"	29"	31"	32"	34"	36"
Cross Back (shoulder to shoulder)	10½"	11½"	11½"	12½"	13"	13½"
Center Back Neck to Cuff	20¾"	21¾"	22¾"	24¾"	26½"	27¾"

Materials

Yarn

570 (655, 785, 875, 985, 1135) yards worsted weight. Model is shown in Summit Hill, by Kraemer Yarns, 3 (3, 4, 4, 5, 6) balls, Greenstone.

Needles

24" circular needle, US size 7 (4.5 mm), or size needed to obtain gauge; 24" circular needle one size smaller for hem, cuffs, and neck and button bands

Other

Stitch markers, stitch holders, tapestry needle, 5 (5, 6, 6, 6, 7) ⅝" buttons

Gauge

20 sts and 26 rows = 4" in stockinet stitch

Notes

1) Please read the Notes, Techniques, and Abbreviations section, p. 120, before you begin.

2) Sweater body is worked flat, as one piece, from hem to underarms, then divided to work back and fronts separately. Sleeves are worked flat from stitches picked up at armhole edges, then seamed and joined to body at underarms. Garter stitch button and neckbands are knitted on last.

Pattern Stitches

Border pattern (for sweater body)

Row 1 (WS) purl
Rows 2-8 knit
Row 9 purl
Rows 10-14 knit
Row 15 purl
Rows 16-17 knit

Border pattern (for sleeves)

Row 1 (WS) knit
Row 2 knit
Row 3 purl
Rows 4-8 knit
Row 9 purl
Rows 10-16 knit
Row 17 purl

Instructions

Cast on at hem: With smaller needle, CO 136 (144, 154, 160, 170, 180) sts. Work 17 rows of border pattern for sweater body.

Body: Switch to larger needle and work in stockinet stitch until sweater measures 11½" (12½", 14½", 15½", 16", 17") from cast-on edge, ending ready to work a RS row.

Divide for back and fronts: On the next row, k25 (29, 28, 31, 32, 34). Keeping those sts on the right-hand needle for the right front, BO 16 (14, 20, 18, 20, 22) sts. Knit to end. On the next row, p25 (29, 28, 31, 32, 34). Keeping those sts on the right-hand needle for the left front, BO 16 (14, 20, 18, 20, 22) sts. There will be 52 (58, 58, 62, 66, 68) sts for the back, and 25 (29, 28, 31, 32, 34) sts for each front section.

Back: Work even in stockinet stitch until back measures 6″ (6½″, 7″, 7½″, 8″, 9″) above underarm bind-off row, ending ready to work a RS row. Knit across the first 12 (15, 15, 16, 18, 18) sts and place them on a stitch holder for the right shoulder. BO the center 28 (28, 28, 30, 30, 32) sts. Knit to end, placing the remaining 12 (15, 15, 16, 18, 18) sts on a stitch holder for the left shoulder.

Right front: Beginning at underarm with a WS row, work in stockinet stitch for 1″. Decrease 1 st at the beginning of every RS row thereafter 13 (13, 10, 12, 9, 9) times, then at the beginning of every 4th

row 0 (1, 3, 3, 5, 7) times, as follows: ssk, k to end. Continue in stockinet stitch on 12 (15, 15, 16, 18, 18) sts until right front measures 6" (6½", 7", 7½", 8", 9") above underarm bind-off row, to match back. Place remaining sts on a stitch holder for right shoulder.

Left front: Beginning at underarm with a RS row, work in stockinet stitch for 1". Decrease 1 st at the end of every RS row thereafter 13 (13, 10, 12, 9, 9) times, then at the end of every 4th row 0 (1, 3, 3, 5, 7) times, as follows: k to last 2 sts, k2tog. Continue in stockinet stitch on 12 (15, 15, 16, 18, 18) sts until left front measures 6" (6½", 7", 7½", 8", 9") above underarm bind-off row, to match right front and back. Place remaining sts on a stitch holder for left shoulder.

Join front to back with a three-needle bind-off at shoulders.

Sleeves: From the RS, using larger needle, leaving underarm bound-off stitches free, pick up and knit 60 (66, 70, 76, 80, 90) sts along the straight armhole edge. Work sleeve in stockinet stitch, beginning with a WS row, decreasing 1 st each side, every 4th row 3 (2, 1, 5, 7, 12) times, then every 6th row 11 (12, 14, 13, 13, 11) times, as follows: k1, ssk, k to last 3 sts, k2tog, k1. Work even in stockinet stitch on 32 (38, 40, 40, 40, 44) sts as necessary until sleeve measures 13" (13½", 14½",

16", 17½", 18½") at center, ending ready to work a WS row. With smaller needle, work 17 rows of border pattern for sleeves. BO.

Sew one-half of the bound-off underarm sts to the top front edge of the sleeve. Sew the other half of the bound-off underarm sts to the top back edge of the sleeve. Sew long under-sleeve seam. Repeat for second sleeve.

Add neck and button bands: With smaller needle, from the RS, beginning at right front hem edge, pick up and knit stitches along right front edge (see Techniques section, p. 121), PM, pick up and knit sts around V-neck, PM, pick up and knit sts along left front edge, ending at hem edge. Work 9 rows of edging, as follows:

Row 1 (WS) k to first marker, sl m, kfb, k to 1 st before next marker, kfb, sl m, k to end
Row 2 knit
Row 3 rep row 1

† Place markers for 5 (5, 6, 6, 6, 7) buttonholes along the stitches for left front band.

Row 4 *knit to buttonhole marker, remove marker, yo, k2tog, rep from * 4 (4, 5, 5, 5, 6) times more, k to end

Row 5 rep row 1

Row 6 rep row 2

Row 7 rep row 1

Row 8 rep row 2

Row 9 BO in knit

† An easy way to do this is to first place a marker about 4 sts up from the hem edge and a second marker about 4 sts down from the neck edge. Now, count the number of sts between these markers. Divide these sts by the number of buttons less 1. If the number of sts does not divide evenly, adjust the number between the top and bottom markers by adding to the center st count, by subtracting from the top or bottom, or by adding one or more stitches to the top or bottom from the center. Once the sts in the center can be evenly divided, place the remaining markers at evenly spaced intervals.

Finishing: Weave in ends and block. Sew buttons to button band opposite buttonholes.

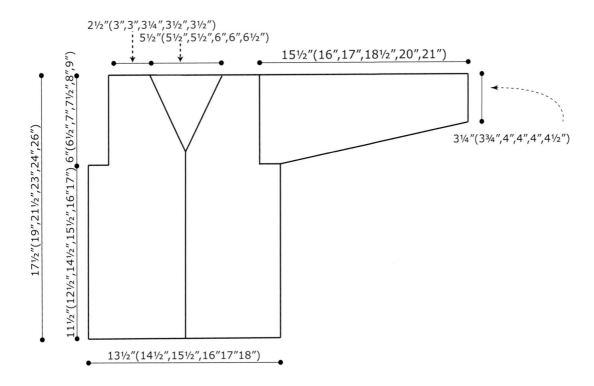

2½"(3",3",3¼",3½",3½")

5½"(5½",5½",6",6",6½")

15½"(16",17",18½",20",21")

17½"(19",21½",23",24",26")

11½"(12½",14½",15½",16"17") 6"(6½",7",7½",8",9")

3¼"(3¾",4",4",4",4½")

13½"(14½",15½",16"17"18")

Turtle

As children, my daughters abhorred turtlenecks and do not usually approve them in their children's wardrobes. This one won approval when I showed how the neck could be used like a turtle pulls its head into its shell to play hide and seek. I loved working this no-sew, top-down sweater and shaping the sleeve caps with short rows. The saddle shoulders make it a very handsome pullover choice.

Measurements

Size	4	6	8	10	12	14
Child's Chest	23″	25″	27″	28″	30″	32″
Finished Sweater:						
Chest	27½″	29″	31½″	32″	33½″	35″
Cross Back (shoulder to shoulder)	10¾″	11¾″	12¾″	13″	14″	14½″
Center Back Neck to Cuff	20″	22¾″	23¾″	26″	28″	29½″

Materials

Yarn

650 (750, 900, 1050, 1150, 1375) yards worsted weight. Model is shown in Tatamy Tweed Worsted, by Kraemer Yarns, 4 (5, 5, 6, 7, 8) balls, Birch.

Needles

24″ and 16″ circular needles, US size 7 (4.5 mm), or size needed to obtain gauge; 16″ circular needle one size smaller for neck trim; additional needles for sleeves (see note on p. 106)

(**Note:** Sleeves are knitted in the round from stitches picked up at the armholes. Although the sleeve can be started on a 16″ circular needle, once decreasing begins it will be necessary to switch to another form of circular knitting. The sleeve can be finished on double-point needles, two 24″ circular needles, or one long circular needle, plus appropriate needles one size smaller for cuffs.)

Other

Stitch markers, stitch holders, tapestry needle

Gauge

20 sts and 24 rows = 4″ in stockinet stitch

Notes

1) Please read the Notes, Techniques, and Abbreviations section, p. 120, before you begin.

2) Sweater is worked top down without sewn seams. Shoulder strips are knitted first. Back and front are worked from stitches picked up along the shoulder strips. Sweater is joined and worked in the round through the hem ribbing. Sleeves are worked from stitches picked up around the armholes. Sleeve caps are shaped with short rows. Sleeves are then worked in the round through cuff ribbing.

Pattern Stitches

Whisper Ribbing (at sweater hem, see also Techniques, p. 121)

On what would be the first round of ribbing, instead of purling every other stitch, purl only every 4th stitch around (a 3 x 1 ribbing). On the next round, begin 1 x 1 ribbing. Don't be concerned on the first round if the numbers don't work out exactly evenly since not every sweater will have a stitch count divisible by 4. Just make sure that you only purl a stitch that will continue to be purled on subsequent rounds of ribbing.

Instructions

Shoulder strips: With larger needle, CO 12 sts. Work even in stockinet stitch until strip measures 3½" (4", 4½", 4½", 5", 5") long, ending ready to work a RS row. BO 1 st at the beginning of the next 2 rows. Break yarn and place remaining 10 sts on a piece of waste yarn to reserve for later. Repeat for second shoulder strip.

Back: From the RS, with larger needle, beginning at the end that has reserved sts, pick up and knit 18 (20, 23, 23, 25, 25) sts along the length of one strip, leaving reserved sts free. Turn and use a cable cast-on (see Techniques, p. 120) to cast on 19 (19, 19, 20, 20, 22) sts (for back of neck). Turn, and, beginning at the cast-on end of the second strip, pick up and knit 18 (20, 23, 23, 25, 25) sts along the length of the strip, ending at the end with reserved sts. There will be 55 (59, 65, 66, 70, 72) sts for the back at the shoulders.

Work even in stockinet stitch for 3" (3½", 4", 4½", 5", 5¼"), ending ready to work a RS row. Work an increase row at the beginning of the next row, and every RS row thereafter 2 (2, 2, 2, 2, 4) times more, as follows: k2, M1R, k to the last 2 sts, M1L, k2. There will be 61 (65, 71, 72, 76, 80) sts following the last increase. Break off.

Place sts for back on waste yarn to reserve for later.

Front

Right shoulder: From the RS, with larger needle, beginning at outside edge (the end that has reserved sts), pick up and knit 18 (20, 23, 23, 25, 25) sts along the front edge of the shoulder strip. Purl one row. Work an increase row on the next row and every RS row thereafter 2 (2, 2, 2, 2, 3) times more, as follows: k to last 2 sts, M1L, k2. There will be 21 (23, 26, 26, 28, 29) sts. Break off.

Left shoulder: From the RS, beginning at neck edge, pick up and knit 18 (20, 23, 23, 25, 25) sts along the front edge of the shoulder strip. Purl one row. Work an increase row on the next row and every RS row thereafter 2 (2, 2, 2, 2, 3) times more, as follows: k2, M1R, k to end. There will be 21 (23, 26, 26, 28, 29) sts. Purl back to center.

Join right and left shoulders: Turn. Use a cable cast-on to CO 13 (13, 13, 14, 14, 14) sts. Purl across sts for right front. There will be 55 (59, 65, 66, 70, 72) sts. Continue working even in stockinet stitch until armhole measures 3" (3½",

4", 4½", 5", 5¼") below shoulder strip, ending ready to work a RS row. Work an increase row at the beginning of the next row, and every RS row thereafter 2 (2, 2, 2, 2, 4) times more, as follows: k2, M1R, k to the last 2 sts, M1L, k2. There will be 61 (65, 71, 72, 76, 80) sts following the last increase.

Body

Join front to back at underarms: Turn. Use a cable cast-on to CO 8 sts at underarm. Join to back and knit across sts for back. Turn. Use a cable cast-on to CO 4 sts at underarm. PM. CO 4 more sts and join to front.

Work even, knitting every round, on 138 (146, 158, 160, 168, 176) sts until sweater body measures 10½" (11", 12½", 14", 14½", 15½") below the underarm join. Work one round of whisper ribbing. Continue in k1/p1 ribbing for 8 rounds. BO loosely in ribbing. (**Note:** body ribbing is worked on the same size needle as the sweater body.)

Sleeves: With larger 16" needle, from the RS, beginning at the center of underarm cast-on sts, pick up and knit 4 sts, then pick up and knit 19 (22, 24, 27, 29, 35) sts, knit across 10 sts of shoulder strip, pick up and knit 19 (22, 24, 27, 29, 35) sts, then pick up and knit remaining 4 sts in underarm cast-on. PM. There will be 56 (62, 66, 72, 76, 88) sts.

Shape sleeve caps: Sleeve caps are shaped with short rows, as follows:

Row 1 k38 (42, 44, 48, 50, 58); wrap the next st and turn
Row 2 p21 (23, 22, 24, 24, 28); wrap the next st and turn
Row 3 knit to the (next) wrapped st, knit the wrapped st, k1, wrap the next st and turn
Row 4 purl to the (next) wrapped st, purl the wrapped st, p1, wrap the next st and turn

(**Note:** Do not knit or purl in the wraps with their corresponding stitches.)

Repeat rows 3 and 4 until the purl row wrap is 4 or 5 sts from the end-of-round marker. Complete the wrap and, on the next row, knit to the end of the round.

Continue in the round on 56 (62, 66, 72, 76, 88) sts, working a decrease round every 6th round 4 (8, 6, 8, 5, 2) times, then every 4th round 8 (5, 8, 8, 13, 19) times, as follows: k1, k2tog, k to the last 3 sts, ssk, k1. Continue working even on 32 (36, 38, 40, 40, 46) sts, until sleeve measures 12½" (14¾", 15¼", 17¼", 18¾", 20") when measured at center. Switch to smaller needles and work one round of whisper ribbing. Then, work 12 rounds of k1/p1 ribbing. BO loosely in ribbing. Repeat for second sleeve.

Box Turtle by Grandma and Luxie

Add neckband: With smaller 16" needle, from the RS, beginning at top of left shoulder, pick up and knit sts around neck (see Techniques section, p. 121), adjusting so that there are an even number of sts. Work in k1/p1 ribbing until turtleneck measures 5½" (5½", 6", 6", 6", 6½"). BO loosely in ribbing.

Finishing: Weave in ends and block.

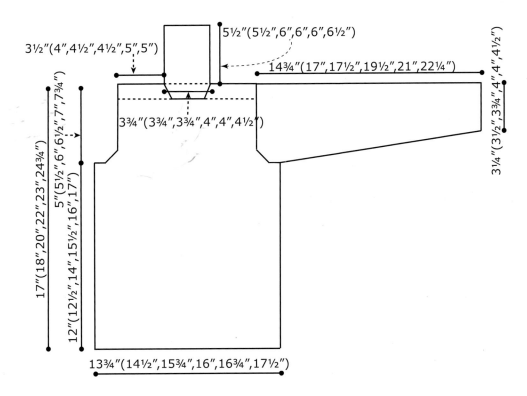

5½"(5½",6",6",6",6½")

3½"(4",4½",4½",5",5")

14¾"(17",17½",19½",21",22¼")

3¾"(3¾",3¾",4",4",4½")

3¼"(3½",3¾",4",4",4½")

17"(18",20",22",23",24¾")

5"(5½",6",6½",7",7¾")

12"(12½",14",15½",16",17")

13¾"(14½",15¾",16",16¾",17½")

Xander

An unpredictable choice of colors adds surprise and fun to this tried and true classic crew neck pullover. Generous ease and neatly fitted sleeves make it comfortable to wear either alone or as a top layer. Let him choose the colors for even more fun.

Measurements

Size	4	6	8	10	12	14
Child's Chest	23″	25″	27″	28″	30″	32″
Finished Sweater:						
Chest	29″	31″	33″	35½″	37½″	40″
Cross Back (shoulder to shoulder)	10½″	11¾″	13″	13¾″	14½″	15¼″
Center Back Neck to Cuff	21″	21¾″	23″	25″	26¾″	27¾″

Materials

Yarn

Color A (orange): 365 (420, 495, 600, 680, 810) yards, and Color B (purple): 100 (105, 110, 120, 125, 135) yards worsted weight. Model is shown in Encore Worsted, by Plymouth Yarn, 2 (3, 3, 3, 4, 5) balls 0175 (Color A) and 1 ball 0454 (Color B).

Needles

24" circular needle, US size 8 (5.0 mm), or size needed to obtain gauge; 16" circular needle one size smaller for cuff and neck ribbing

Other

Stitch markers, stitch holders, tapestry needle

Gauge

18 sts and 24 rows = 4″ in stockinet stitch

Notes

1) Please read the Notes, Techniques, and Abbreviations section, p. 120, before you begin.

2) Sweater body is worked in the round from hem to underarms, and then divided to work back and front separately. Sleeves are worked flat, separately, then sewn to body and seamed. Neckband is knitted on last.

Pattern Stitches

Ribbing (for hem and neckband)

(all rounds) p1, *k3, p2, rep from *, ending last rep with p1

Ribbing (for cuffs)

Row 1 (WS) p2, *k2, p3, rep from *, ending last rep with p2

Row 2 (RS) k2, *p2, k3, rep from *, ending last rep with k2

Whisper Ribbing (at hem and cuffs, see also Techniques, p. 121)

(at the hem) *p1, k4, rep from * around; and (at the cuffs) k3, p1, *k4, p1, rep from *, ending k2

Instructions

Cast on at hem: With Color B and larger needle, CO 130 (140, 150, 160, 170, 180) sts. Join in a round, PM, and work in ribbing pattern for hem for 7 rounds. Work 1 round of whisper ribbing. Knit with Color B for 4 rounds more.

Body: Continuing in stockinet stitch, work the following stripe sequence:

Color A 2 rounds
Color B 8 rounds
Color A 4 rounds
Color B 6 rounds
Color A 6 rounds
Color B 4 rounds
Color A 8 rounds
Color B 2 rounds

The remainder of the sweater is worked in Color A. Work in stockinet stitch until sweater measures 12½" (13½", 15", 16½", 17", 18") from cast-on edge.

Divide for back and front: Knit 61 (66, 71, 76, 80, 85); BO 8 (8, 8, 8, 10, 10); k56 (61, 66, 71, 74, 79); BO 8 (8, 8, 8, 10, 10). There will be 57 (62, 67, 72, 75, 80) sts for the back and 57 (62, 67, 72, 75, 80) sts for the front.

Back: Knit across sts for back. Turn. Continue in stockinet stitch, decreasing 1 st each side, every RS row, 4 (4, 4, 5, 5, 6) times, as follows: ssk, k to last 2 sts, k2tog. Work even on 49 (54, 59, 62, 65,

68) sts until armhole measures 5″ (5½″, 6″, 6½″, 7″, 8″) above underarm bind-off row, ending ready to work a RS row. Knit across first 12 (14, 16, 18, 19, 20) sts and place them on a stitch holder for right shoulder. Knit across next 25 (26, 27, 26, 27, 28) sts and place them on a stitch holder for back neck. Knit to end, placing 12 (14, 16, 18, 19, 20) sts on a stitch holder for left shoulder.

Front: Beginning with a WS row, purl across sts for front. Decrease 1 st each side, every RS row, 4 (4, 4, 5, 5, 6) times, as follows: ssk, k to last 2 sts, k2tog. Work even on 49 (54, 59, 62, 65, 68) sts until armhole measures 2½″ (3″, 3″, 3½″, 4″, 5″) above underarm bind-off row, ending ready to work a RS row. Knit across 18 (20, 23, 25, 26, 27) sts for left front. Knit across 13 (14, 13, 12, 13, 14) sts for center front and place them on a stitch holder. Knit to end (18 [20, 23, 25, 26, 27] sts for right front).

Right front and shoulder: Continue in stockinet stitch, decreasing 1 st at neck edge, every RS row 6 (6, 7, 7, 7, 7) times, as follows: ssk, k to end. Work even on 12 (14, 16, 18, 19, 20) sts until armhole measures 5″ (5½″, 6″, 6½″, 7″, 8″) above underarm bind-off row, to match back. Place remaining sts on a stitch holder for right shoulder.

Left front and shoulder: Beginning at neck edge with a WS row, continue in stockinet stitch, decreasing 1 st at neck edge, every RS row, 6 (6, 7, 7, 7, 7) times, as follows: k to last 2 sts, k2tog. Work even on 12 (14, 16, 18, 19, 20) sts until armhole measures 5″ (5½″, 6″, 6½″, 7″, 8″) above underarm bind-off row, to match back and right front. Place remaining sts on a stitch holder for left shoulder.

Join front to back with a three-needle bind-off at shoulders.

Sleeves: With Color A and smaller needle, CO 31 (36, 36, 36, 41, 41) sts. Work in ribbing pattern for cuffs for 11 rows. Switch to larger needle and work 1 row of whisper ribbing. Continue in stockinet stitch, increasing 1 st each side every 8th (8th, 6th, 6th, 6th, 6th) row 7 (7, 9, 11, 11, 7) times, then every 4th row 0 (0, 0, 0, 0, 8) times, as follows: k1, kfb, k to last 3 sts, kfb, k2. Work even on 45 (50, 54, 58, 63, 71) sts until sleeve measures 12½″ (12½″, 12½″, 14″, 15″, 15¼″) from cast-on edge, measured at center, ending ready to work a RS row. BO 5 (5, 5, 5, 6, 6) sts at the beginning of the next two rows. Decrease 1 st each side, every RS row, 4 (4, 4, 5, 5, 6) times, as follows: ssk, k to last 2 sts, k2tog. Purl one row. Then

decrease 1 st each side, every row 5 (7, 9, 9, 11, 12) times, as follows: (RS rows) ssk, k to last 2 sts, k2tog; (WS rows) p2tog, p to last 2 sts, ssp. BO 1 (2, 2, 2, 2, 3) sts at the beginning of the next 4 rows. BO remaining 13 (10, 10, 12, 11, 11) sts. Repeat for second sleeve.

Add neckband: Beginning at left shoulder seam, from the RS, with smaller needle, pick up and knit stitches along left front neck edge (see Techniques section, p. 121). Knit across stitches from center front stitch holder. Pick up and knit stitches along right front neck edge. Knit across stitches from back neck stitch holder. Adjust stitches to a multiple of 5 and work in ribbing pattern for hem and neckband for 7 rounds. BO loosely in pattern.

Finishing: Block sleeves and body. Sew sleeves to armholes. Sew under-sleeve seams, from armhole to cuff. Weave in ends.

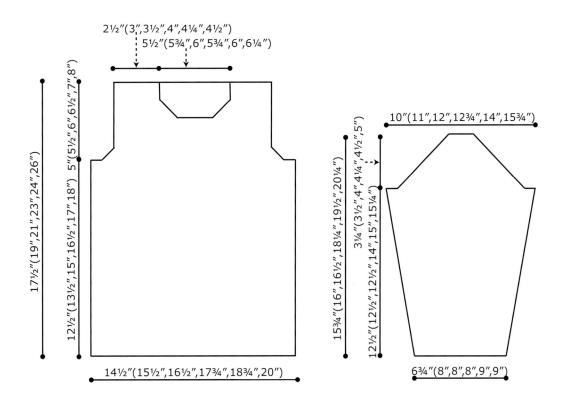

2½"(3",3½",4",4¼",4½")

5½"(5¾",6",5¾",6",6¼")

17½"(19",21",23",24",26")

12½"(13½",15",16½",17",18")

5"(5½",6",6½",7",8")

14½"(15½",16½",17¾",18¾",20")

10"(11",12",12¾",14",15¾")

15¾"(16",16½",18¼",19½",20¼")

3¼"(3½",4",4¼",4½",5")

12½"(12½",12½",14",15",15¼")

6¾"(8",8",8",9",9")

Notes, Techniques, & Abbreviations

Notes

1) Before you begin, please check our web site (TimelessKnitsPublications.com) for corrections to the published instructions.

2) Instructions are given for size 4, with (6, 8, 10, 12, 14) in parentheses. If only one number is given, it is for all sizes.

3) Selvedge stitches have been included to allow for seaming where required. Measurements shown in schematics are prior to seaming and finishing.

Techniques

1) **Attached I-cord:** Start by picking up stitches along the edge to which the I-cord is to be attached. Break the yarn and begin with the first stitch picked up. For a 2-st attached I-cord, knit the first stitch; for a 3-st attached I-cord, knit the first 2 sts. The next stitch is knit together with the following stitch, through the back loops. Replace sts from right-hand needle to left-hand needle. Repeat for each row of I-cord. Bind off to finish. (**Note:** Another technique requires that you cast on sts before you begin. For a 2-st I-cord, cast on 2 sts; for a 3-st I-cord, cast on 3 sts; then work the I-cord as above. I prefer to skip this step because my results are approximately the same.)

2) **Cable cast-on** (with work in progress): *Insert the right-hand needle between the first two stitches on the left-hand needle, wrap the right-hand needle tip as if to knit, pull a loop through and place this loop onto the left-hand needle to make a new stitch, rep from * until the desired number of sts have been cast on.

3) **Garter stitch** is produced by knitting every row (when knitting flat), or alternating knit with purl rounds (when knitting in the round).

4) **I-cord** is worked on 2 double-pointed needles. Cast on the specified number of sts. Do not turn work. Slide the stitches to the other end of the needle such that the first stitch you will knit is at the opposite end of the stitches from the working yarn. Knit all the stitches, applying extra tension to the first stitch to pull the yarn across the back. Slide the stitches again,

give the cord end a tug, pull the yarn across the back, and knit the next row. Repeat this process until the cord is the desired length.

5) **Pick up and knit stitches:** Unless instructed otherwise, pick up and knit sts at a ratio of 1 st for each st in straight hem edges and back neck edge, 3 sts for every 4 sts along shaped edges, and 3 sts for every 4 rows along center fronts. To pick up and knit sts along a straight armhole edge, pick up and knit sts at the ratio that is the same as that of stitches per inch to rows per inch.

6) **Stockinet stitch** is produced by alternating knit and purl rows (when knitting flat), or knitting every round (when knitting in the round).

7) **Three-needle bind-off:** If necessary, move the stitches from their stitch holders to appropriately sized needles. Unless directed otherwise, place the garment pieces right sides together. With a third needle, knit one stitch through the first stitch on both needles. Now repeat, knitting a second stitch through the second stitch on both needles. Pull the first stitch knit over the second stitch, as for a regular bind-off, and continue across the row until all stitches are bound off.

8) **Whisper ribbing:** The transition between stockinet stitch and a ribbed band is often too harsh to look natural. Sometimes a ribbed band will have a tendency to flip up as well. I've devised a transition to/from the ribbing, that I call whisper ribbing. It works well functionally and visually. Instructions for each instance where this technique is used appear in the Pattern Stitches section of the individual pattern.

9) **Work in established pattern:** Once a stitch pattern has been established on previous rows, subsequent rows may require that stitches be added or subtracted to/from the stitch count. To work in established pattern, start each modified row with the appropriate stitch in the stitch pattern instructions that would maintain the stitch pattern in a presentation consistent with previously executed rows.

10) **Wrap a stitch:** In shaping with short rows, it is sometimes necessary to wrap a stitch before turning to prevent a hole in the knitting where the row ended short. On a knit row, knit to the directed point in the row; then, bring the working yarn to the front of the work between the needles. Slip the next stitch (as if to purl) from the left-hand needle to the right-hand needle. Take the working yarn to the back of the work between the needles. Finish by replacing the slipped and wrapped stitch back to the left-hand needle without twisting. On a purl row, purl to the directed point in the row; then, take the working yarn to the back of the work between the needles. Slip the next stitch (as if to purl) from the left-hand needle to the right-hand needle. Bring the working yarn to the front of the work between the needles. Finish by replacing the slipped and wrapped stitch back to the left-hand needle without twisting. The wraps sometimes get worked together with their corresponding stitches when the short rows are completed.

Abbreviations

BO: Bind off

CC: Contrast color

CO: Cast on

k: Knit

k2tog: Knit 2 stitches together—a right-slanting decrease

kfb: Knit in the front and the back of the same stitch—an increase

M1L (make one—left slanting)**:** Bring the tip of the left-hand needle under the strand between needles, from front to back. Knit through the back of the loop.

M1R (make one—right slanting)**:** Bring the tip of the left-hand needle under the strand between needles, from back to front. Knit this loop.

MC: Main color

p: Purl

p2tog: Purl two stitches together—a right-slanting decrease

pfb: Purl in the front and back of the stitch—an increase

PM: Place marker

rep: Repeat

RS: Right side

sl1: Slip one stitch (without twisting)

sl m: Slip marker

ssk (slip, slip, knit—a left-slanting decrease): Slip two stitches individually from left to right needle, as if to knit. Place tip of left needle through front loops of both slipped stitches and knit them together.

ssp (slip, slip, purl—a left-slanting decrease): Slip two stitches individually from left to right needle, as if to knit. Place them back on the left-hand needle, without twisting. Purl them together through the back loops.

st / sts: Stitch / stitches

tbl: Through the back loop(s)

WS: Wrong side

wyif (with yarn in front): Bring the yarn to the front of the work, between the needles (toward you, regardless of which is the right side); follow the stitch instruction; take the yarn to the back of the work.

yo (yarn over—an increase): For a yarn over between knit stitches, bring the yarn to the front of the work between the needle tips. Knit the next stitch by taking the yarn to the back, over the top of the right-hand needle. For a yarn over between purl stitches, take the yarn to the back of the work over the top of the right-hand needle. Bring the yarn to the front of the work under the right-hand needle and purl the next stitch.

Yarns and Notions

Yarns

220 Superwash
Cascade Yarns
100% Superwash wool
100 grams/3.5 ounces
220 yards
(Cotton Candy and Head of the Class)

Encore Worsted
Plymouth Yarn
75% acrylic, 25% wool
100 grams/3.5 ounces
200 yards
(Tic-Tac-Toe, Vested, and Xander)

Greenland
Cascade Yarns
100% merino Superwash
100 grams/3.5 ounces
137 yards
(Rib Tickler)

Perfection
Kraemer Yarns
30% domestic merino, 70% acrylic
100 grams/3.5 ounces
225 yards
(Beachcomber)

Summit Hill
Kraemer Yarns
100% merino Superwash wool
100 grams/3.5 ounces
230 yards
(Skip)

Tatamy Tweed Worsted
Kraemer Yarns
40% cotton, 60% acrylic
100 grams/3.5 ounces
180 yards
(Camp Jacket, Old Sport, Turtle, and Willow)

Buttons

JHB
#10004
(Tic-Tac-Toe)

#45144
(Head of the Class)

la-petite
#526
(Skip)

Acknowledgments

The idea to write and publish this book was born in the wonderfully inspirational and supportive circle created by Cat Bordhi and her Visionary Retreats. The infant book was nurtured and grew to maturity through Cat's mentorship and the support of fellow visionaries, most especially Janel Laidman, Cookie A, Carol Breitner, and Margaret Fisher.

No book gets published without the efforts of a great many behind-the-scenes experts and I had the good fortune to work with a talented and fun production team. My heartfelt thanks go to Clara Masessa (test and sample knitter), Matthew Bellavia (copy editor), Carol Breitner (insightful reader), Janel Laidman (book designer extraordinaire), and John de Longpré (life partner and coach, without whose patient support I could not have persevered).

To Ron and Ginny Weerstra, who generously open their comfortable home to me as a photo studio whenever I ask, my gratitude and most sincere appreciation.

Thank you to Jean Dunbabin (Cascade Yarns), David Schmidt (Kraemer Yarns), and JoAnne Turcotte (Plymouth Yarn) for supplying the yarn.

Finally, and most humbly, thank you Gini, Elli, Luxie, JJ, Lyzzie, and Caleb. You inspire me every day in every way.

About the Author

Photo: Dawn Wiltzer

Chris de Longpré is the creative force behind Knitting At KNoon Designs, LLC, designing and publishing popular knitting patterns since 2003. Her patterns are known and loved for their whimsy and their clarity in instruction. Timeless Knits for Kids (Size 4-14) is her first published collection for children.

You can see more of Chris's work at www.KnittingAtKNoon.com.